A Practical Guide to Puppy Raising

Nurture Your Dog the Ideal Way

Book 1 of the Furry Friends Series

Max Parrott

Legal & Disclaimer

The information contained in this book and its contents is not designed to replace or take the place of any form of medical or professional advice; and is not meant to replace the need for independent medical, financial, legal or other professional advice or services, as may be required. The content and information in this book has been provided for educational and entertainment purposes only.

The content and information contained in this book has been compiled from sources deemed reliable, and it is accurate to the best of the Author's knowledge, information and belief. However, the Author cannot guarantee its accuracy and validity and cannot be held liable for any errors and/or omissions. Further, changes are periodically made to this book as and when needed. Where appropriate and/or necessary, you must consult a professional (including but not limited to your doctor, attorney, financial advisor or such other professional advisor) before using any of the suggested remedies, techniques, or information in this book.

Upon using the contents and information contained in this book, you agree to hold harmless the Author from and against any damages, costs, and expenses, including any legal fees potentially resulting from the application of any of the information provided by this book. This disclaimer applies to any loss, damages or injury caused by the use and application, whether directly or indirectly, of any advice or information presented, whether for breach of contract, tort, negligence, personal injury, criminal intent, or under any other cause of action.

You agree to accept all risks of using the information presented inside this book.

You agree that by continuing to read this book, where appropriate and/or necessary, you shall consult a professional (including but not limited to your doctor, attorney, or financial advisor or such other advisor as needed) before using any of the suggested remedies, techniques, or information in this book.

Table of Contents

Introduction

Congratulations! So, you've decided to bring home a new furry friend. Being a puppy-parent and eventual dog owner is one of the most fun and rewarding things you'll ever do. New puppy care should be fun but if you're a first-time owner, those early weeks can easily become more of a challenge than a joy. As a new puppy owner, you will be aware of the responsibilities that come with caring and rearing your new pet. As such, taking care of your puppy requires a lot of time, patience, love, and money. Yes, these lovable canine friends can be very expensive, and you'd want to make the most of how you allocate your resources into giving them the best care they can possibly have. Once you bring your new puppy home, there seems to be a thousand things you need to know all at once!

This book is aimed at first-time puppy owners like you, who are looking for practical ways for raising dogs. I will help guide you every step of the way with useful tips and tricks from getting your little furball settled, to teaching them basic training. Within the chapters of this book, you will find a wealth of invaluable information, and with the correct level of training, planning, love, and attention, your puppy will be the perfect companion for many years to come.

Chapter 1 – Before Taking Your Puppy Home

Are you ready for a puppy?

Puppies aren't just cute and cuddly – they're also demanding, fragile, sensitive, destructive, loud, exhaustive, exasperating, and expensive! It's basically like raising a child, with all the same highs and lows, with the difference being their development is much more condensed in a shorter time frame.

Before you consider getting a new puppy, here are a few things you need to keep in mind:

Time to train and socialize the new pooch

Bringing home a dog doesn't mean you can choose when to show attention to your pet at your own convenience. A new puppy especially needs extra care and attention, much like a newborn baby. Your commitment should extend beyond your comfort zone, beyond usual sleeping times, and beyond puppyhood. It is a partnership that can potentially last much longer than you would initially imagine. While that's not a bad thing, this means that you should never falter at any point in giving quality care and attention to your dog. Commit to teaching him the rules of your home – potty training, socialisation with other dogs, and exercise, among others. A healthy dog is reflective of the kind of love and care the master gives. Make sure yours can stand out in the most positive way.

Commitment to having a pet for the next decade or longer

Getting a new puppy that can grow into an adult dog might be a big problem for commitment-phobes. Dogs can stay around typically for the next 10, 12 or 15 years, and if you're lucky, even longer. This long-term obligation may easily survive other relationships you may have, so make sure you are prepared to be in it for the long run.

Studying up on care and safety of dogs

Give yourself plenty of time to learn about nutrition, exercise, training, and health issues that pertain to your dog. Keep yourself informed as it can make your life and your canine friend's life much easier when you take him home.

Financial capability of keeping a dog

Let's face it, owning a dog is expensive. There are yearly vaccinations and check-ups, de-worming schedules, daily food expenses, formal training, insurance, veterinary visits, etc. – and these are just the tip of the iceberg! While they may not need a $100,000 college tuition, you still need to make sure you can keep up their demands in order to ensure a comfortable life for your pet.

Your Lifestyle, Schedule and Environment

If you are a retired senior looking for a laid-back companion that doesn't need too much exercise, a border collie may not be your best bet. Likewise, if you're an athlete, you may not want to get a pug. Before getting a dog, choose the breed, whether pure or mixed, that fits into your lifestyle. Factor in working hours, energy levels of the puppy, and family circumstances. Will a barking puppy disturb the neighbours, or do you live alone on your floor? Can a giant breed squeeze into your apartment? Do you travel often for business and can you leave your dog for long periods of time? Take all these things into consideration and do your research on what breed best suits you.

The Cost of Keeping a Dog

Why does it matter to know the costs of owning a dog? After all, we all love our pets and we wouldn't want to put a price tag on them. But the hard truth is that pets can be costly, and it helps for us to adjust not only to their daily needs but also for the unforeseen and emergency expenses they may incur during their lifetime with us. People, in general, do not usually realise that rearing puppies involves a lot of time, effort, expense and commitment. Not planning this carefully can often lead to dogs eventually leading a life of misery, one that is deprived of socialisation, love, care and basic needs.

Some of the expenses you need to prepare for include food bills, corresponding vet bills, dog bed or crate, occasional treats and chew bones, food and water bowls, collars and leash, vitamins, grooming accessories, stain removers and training aids. All these should be factored in on top of the purchase price of the puppy. You can also do the dog community a huge favor by adopting instead.

Chapter 2 – Preparing for Your Puppy

At last, the puppy you've wanted for so long is finally home. This is an exciting time for you; but for your pet, it can be a very stressful adjustment. Your new puppy will be leaving the security of their mother and littermates. They will be experiencing new sights, sounds, and smells - unfamiliar ones at that. In order to prepare for this transition, here are a couple of tips you need to do in order to get your puppy settled in your new home.

Essential Supplies

Stainless steel bowls for food and water

Provide durable bowls for your teething puppies as these can withstand rust, breakages or chips. Puppies will naturally bite and chew anything in sight, which can be a big problem when using plastic bowls. Plus, stainless bowls are more sanitary. Find a permanent place for these food bowls so that the puppy develops the familiar routine of going to where the food and water are when he needs them.

Sleeping place

Giving your puppy their own safe place to sleep on is essential in making them feel secure, take refuge and sleep. Provide a comfortable bed or a puppy crate in the corner.

Collar and leash

In order to get your puppy used to wearing a leash and collar, you need to start using them right away. Make sure that the collar is snug enough not to slip over his head, but not too tight. You can also provide a dog tag for identification.

Brush and comb

You want your puppy to grow up being familiar with handling by different people, and grooming is the easiest way to do that. It can also make brushing and combing easier for both of you as your puppy grows bigger and stronger. This will also save you a lot of hassle when your dear one goes to the vet for general checkups or vaccinations.

Puppy toys

Choose a toy that is very durable. Purchase rubber toys that are smaller than your puppies for teething purposes, and larger size ones for larger puppies. Choose only safe toys, and discard or throw out the ones that already show signs of wear and tear. In order to encourage them to play with their toys, you should set aside some playtime to get your puppy's attention – and this will also function as invaluable bonding time. Playtime can be used as an alternative to food treats as it is also a valuable reward. Remember, puppies want nothing more than to spend as much time as they can with their master, so this can function as positive reinforcement.

Treats

Just like humans, dogs are social creatures. To facilitate bonding between you and your furry friend, keep treats in handy. These are an effective and appropriate training tool and a great way to say, "Well-done," in terms your dog clearly understands.

Stain and odour remover

Dogs can leave stains and odours they may not know about and this is an inevitable part of living with them. There are a variety of effective cleaning products that help you deal with this. Know which ones work for you and remember to choose the ones that are specifically formulated for the use of pets. Using these after a puppy has done his business in the wrong area will erase the scent and lessen the likelihood of a repeat occurrence.

Other optional items include:

- ID tag
- Crate
- Dog shampoo

- Puppy/Dog training pads

- Clippers

- Dog flea treatment

- Kennels for outdoor use

- Pet gates for indoors

- Muzzles

- Grooming products and accessories

Chapter 3 - Welcoming Your Puppy Home

The Indoor Setup

- Electrical cords should be wrapped or hidden to prevent them from being chewed on. Protect your puppy from accidental shock and burns to the mouth.

- Limit access to items you don't want your puppy to have

- Store small and undesirable items inside closets or cupboards with a door you can keep closed

- Store away harmful cleaning products where your puppy can't get to them

- Keep your trash under wraps. Left to their own devices, a curious new puppy can ingest something toxic from your trash bin that's left uncovered, causing an internal obstruction or even suffocation when their head gets caught in a bag.

- Keep your medications away from where your puppy can reach them, as these drugs may get ingested and cause poisoning or other side effects. Don't leave them lying on top of nightstands, or countertops. Instead, transfer them to a secure cabinet or drawer.

- Razors, pills, cotton swabs and soap left within your dog's reach can easily be ingested. The bathroom should be kept free from these items or store them where they are not visible to your puppy.

- Keep the toilet cover down at all times. A curious puppy could easily jump into the toilet bowl and get stuck.

- Many puppies like to den under the bed and wedge themselves behind furniture, so put temporary blockades to prevent them from hiding where they shouldn't.

The Outdoor Setup

- Inspect your lawn for holes or gaps in your fence where your puppy could escape. Make sure your fences are high enough to prevent your dog from getting over them.

- If you have fencing without a flat top, they can be a hazard for dogs hanging themselves on their collars or impaling themselves on metal spikes or wood. You may have to replace these depending on the situation and the nature of the puppy. Check also for protruding nails, screws or wire that may injure the puppy.

- Remove all chemical fertilisers, herbicides, insecticides, and poisonous plants.

- Ask your veterinarian for a list of plants your puppy should stay away from.

- As your puppy may try to escape from your yard and bolt out, install self-closing hinges on all gates with proper locks. Self-closing or lockable gates that only family members can open are a really solid safety net.

- If you have a pond or a pool, it's wise to fence these off until your puppy has grown and proven to be an able swimmer. Although dogs are natural swimmers, it is important to keep an eye on them just in case something happens.

- Set limits. Your puppy is naturally curious and is bound to explore as much as they can and test their limits. Set up baby gates or pens and close appropriate doors to keep your puppy from getting into and out of places you don't want them to.

- Keep your puppy grounded. Puppies can be very clumsy and have the tendency to be at risk of injury when jumping off high places when they're young.

A Comfortable Sleeping Space

Where should my Puppy sleep?

First of all, think about where you want your future adult dog to sleep. If you want him in your room, then you can set up a crate for him beside you. If you want him in the living room, think about moving the crate to that area after the first couple of nights.

Although there's nothing wrong with allowing your puppy to sleep next to you in bed, it is recommended that you wait at least until he is six months old and potty trained. If you are putting him inside a crate, you may need to get up every 4 hours at least in order to let your puppy out for a potty break, at least for the first two weeks or so. Toilet and crate training tips will be discussed in more detail in the next few chapters.

What if the puppy won't stop crying?

It is natural for the puppy to whine or cry during the first few nights. As hard as this may be, it is recommended that you ignore this. Just have the crate beside you so he can see you and you can give an occasional reassuring pat every now and then. In a few weeks, he will learn to adjust.

Food and Nutrition

Caring for your puppy means that you need to supply them with quality food that gives them energy, build up their immune system, promote growth and prevent health-related problems. To do this, you need to invest in quality food that has sufficient vitamins, minerals, proteins, carbohydrates and fats needed by the puppy's growing body. Otherwise, any deficiency in these important components could lead to malnutrition or joint problems. Improper growth can lead to long-term damage to their health and well-being.

It may be tempting to give your puppy table scraps every now and then, and it may even feel like you're giving him a treat, but in reality – you're not. What you're actually doing is upsetting the balance of his diet, leading him to suffer from obesity and also encourage him to disturb you during your mealtimes. Instead, provide your puppy with a specially formulated dog food that is made especially for his unique needs. This way, you can ensure you are giving him the proper and right nutrition he needs.

How to Feed Your Puppy

The breed and size of your puppy are two things you need to consider when determining their nutritional needs. Adult dog sizes are classified into four types: mini, medium, maxi, and giant. Mini dogs grow to an average adult weight of 1-10kg, medium dogs at 11-25 kg, maxi dogs at 26-44kg, and giant dogs at 45kg and up. Determine the breed of your dog and the eventual size he grows into. Some dog food brands are specifically formulated to a particular breed, and if you can invest in these, it is wise to do so. Mini dogs require three meals a day from birth to four months old, and only two meals a day from five months onwards. On the other hand, medium, maxi, and giant dogs should be given three meals a day from birth to six months, then two meals a day from seven months onwards.

Small but scheduled meals are ideal for your puppy. Allow them to eat from the same bowl and at the same place every time. Remember, when it comes to puppies, routine is key. Make sure not to overfeed your puppy.

You can check the recommended feeding guidelines as shown on the packaging of your chosen dog food brand.

Always provide clean and fresh water at all times. Because active puppies tend to play a lot with it, change the water regularly.

Your growing puppy's nutritional needs will eventually change as he transitions into adulthood. Sometimes, you need to change his food a couple of times in order to cope with these changes and still ensure that he gets the nutrients he needs. Food transition is ideally done over a 7-day period, by gradually mixing the existing food with the new food until the end of the week. This ensures that this change will be gentle on his bowels as puppies have very sensitive stomachs.

Starting on the first two days, mix about 75% of the old food with 25% of the new food. By the next two days - days three and four - each mealtime should consist of half the new food and half of the old food. On the fifth and sixth days, the new food should be more than the old food, at a ratio of 75% for the former and 25% for the latter. By the seventh day, you will have only the new food to give to your furry little friend, rendering the transition complete.

Exercise

It is common for puppies to be full of energy. This is why it is crucial for you to pay attention to their individual needs when it comes to exercise and play.

Contrary to their energetic nature however, puppies need less exercise than fully-grown dogs. This is because these balls of energy are at risk of over-exercising, which may lead to injuries to their still-developing joints and limbs. Since their musculoskeletal structure is still soft, they can easily be damaged. An ideal length would be five minutes of exercise per month of age, to begin with, extending to longer times when they are adults.

All dogs, regardless of their breed, should have one walk per day. This helps to strengthen their muscles and bones. It also helps to reduce blood pressure and avoid obesity. Never push your puppy to their limits when they begin to show signs of being tired and worn out. Always ensure that you have enough water to provide for your puppy and try to walk in cooler areas on hot days.

Be consistent in your exercise or walking schedule. A regular pattern will help with their natural development into a full-grown dog. Be responsible. Remember to take poop bags with you and clean up after your pet and keep the landscape clean for other people.

Do not exercise your pup after eating or with a full stomach as this may cause bloating. Watch out for signs of overheating such as your puppy panting excessively, drooling, showing signs of agitation or confusion, or vomiting. If this happens, move them to a cooler place; apply cool water to their skin, belly, and under their legs, and fan them.

If you're walking in the snow, avoid roads that have been treated with salt as these can sting your puppy's feet. There is also cause for stomach upset if they lick their paws. Avoid any forced exercise such as: jogging or running with a puppy, excessive ball or Frisbee throwing and catching, running your puppy alongside your bike, or taking fast-paced or long walks.

On the Lead

One of the many ways you can allow your puppy to exercise is while on the lead. Here are the do's and don'ts:

- Walk your pet at a normal walking pace.

- Stop to rest if your pet rests or lies down during the walk, then continue walking when they are ready to walk again.

- Stop the walk and return home once your puppy seems too tired to continue.

Off the Lead

Another form of exercise you can do is to let your puppy off the lead. Here's a bit of advice if you prefer it that way:

- Allow your pet to run freely, and in a safe environment. This way, they can regulate their own pace and the amount of exercise they get. Try to ensure that this is an enclosed area so that your puppy does not wander too far off. The good news is they will probably stay near, to begin with, as they are still unfamiliar with their surroundings.

- Don't over-exercise your pet by doing too much ball or Frisbee throwing and catching.

Although walking is a great activity to get your puppy strong and healthy, it is also believed to help them gain social benefits. Puppies that are regularly walked are shown to be friendlier and more approachable to others.

Injections and Vaccinations

To provide relevant protection, your puppy should be vaccinated at the earliest stage possible. Getting your puppy vaccinated will give you peace of mind and prevent your dog from becoming seriously ill. In addition to keeping them immune, you will be protecting the spread of infection to other animals too.

Your Puppy's First Vaccine Shots

The responsibilities of puppy-owners are not limited to food and shelter, but also in ensuring their furry friends gets vaccinated against diseases. Medical records should be secured whether you are purchasing or adopting a puppy. Trips to your veterinarian will be more often in the first year of puppyhood, as regular booster shots and immunizations are required at this stage.

When puppies are born, they get their initial immunity from their mothers, passed on through her milk. When they are weaned, that immunity is also stopped. This is why the best and most effective time for vaccines to work is when your puppy has been properly weaned off from its mother. Your vet will then determine what immunisations are needed for your dog. Factors like the number of household pets you have or the place you live in will come into consideration.

Scheduling Vaccines

Most of a puppy's vaccinations are given at six to eight weeks. There are two-or-three-week intervals in between, and by the time they are 14 weeks old, they will have received the majority of their much-needed immunisations. Some common vaccines include those against parvovirus, herpes, hepatitis, and distemper. Rabies shots are also a must, although different states may have different scheduling. There are vaccines that are given in combination, containing three or more vaccines in one go, while others are given alone.

Ideally, puppies should be up to date on shots by the time they reach 16 weeks old, otherwise, you may need to see your vet to start another schedule. The vet may require you to start the shots all over again if you're not sure or if no records of previous immunisations have been documented.

Some of the vaccines that can be given as early as six to14 weeks are DHLPPC, Bordetella, Giardia, and Lyme. Rabies vaccines can start at around 16 weeks. Your vet will then determine the next follow-up shots and boosters thereafter.

Remember that different states have different regulations and different breeds may require different shots and schedules. Always consult your vet for any further clarification.

When a puppy is finished with their initial "puppy shot" series, they're not completely done with their vaccines. Booster vaccinations will be needed throughout your dog's life. The frequency and types of vaccine boosters your dog will need depends on their lifestyle, where you live and travel to with them, how common certain diseases are in your area, and a host of other factors. Ask your vet for a specific list of these recommended boosters.

How to Recognise Infections

In the event where your dog has not been vaccinated, it is important that you know how to spot any potential signs of disease right away. Some early signs of infection include diarrhoea, fever, cough, laboured breathing, vomiting, lethargy, loss of appetite, drooling, and pale tongue, gums, and nose among others. These symptoms can be signals of an underlying disease, and it is best to rush your puppy to your vet as soon as possible.

Worming

Puppies are at an increased risk from worms, as this can easily be passed down from the mother to the puppy during pregnancy. Puppies with worm infestations can experience stomach problems, sickness, weight loss, and other serious problems. It is advised that you de-worm your puppy from two to three weeks of age, at every two-week interval, until three months of age. Puppies are de-wormed every month at this age until six months, which then increases to every four months thereafter. It is important to keep a log so that you can keep track of the important dates.

Fleas

Fleas are a common menace in domestic pets, puppies included. Fleas live by feeding on the blood of your animal. This can be very painful and will cause health problems for young puppies, so utmost protection is crucial. One of the main problems with fleas is that they are hard to detect. They burrow inside the fur of your pet and leech from there. The easiest way to detect them is to look for dark specks on your puppy's coat and if these specks turn brown or red, it is very likely your pet has fleas. These specks are basically dried blood on which the fleas have been feeding on.

Spaying and Neutering

What is the difference between spay and neuter?

A spay is a veterinary surgical procedure that involves the removal of the female dog's uterus and both ovaries. On the other hand, neutering or castration is the surgical removal of a dog's testes.

Female dogs should be spayed between three and nine months old to reduce the risk of breast cancer and incontinence problems.

Male dogs should be neutered between six and nine months to reduce the risk of testicular cancer and to calm aggression.

Although these procedures can be done to young puppies, dog owners should always consult with the veterinarian to determine the best age to do so.

Benefits of Spaying and Neutering

- Spaying your female puppy helps prevent uterine infections and breast tumours.

- Neutering males helps prevent testicular cancer and some prostate problems.

- Spayed dogs won't yowl or urinate all over the place, while neutered males will be less likely to roam away from home.

- Spaying or neutering is a responsible way of preventing unwanted puppies caused by accidental breeding.

- The cost of spaying/neutering is far less than the cost of having a litter.

Tips Before and After Surgery

Your vet will usually give you pre-surgery instructions to follow. While an adult dog should not be given any food or drink the night before surgery, your puppy needs adequate nutrition and the vet may recommend the food not to be withheld. Provide your pet a quiet place to recover indoors away from other pets.

Prevent your puppy from running or jumping for up to two weeks or until the advice from the vet. Prevent your pet from licking the surgical wound as this may cause infection. If needed, an Elizabethan collar may be used. Avoid giving a bath to your pet for at least 10 days post-surgery.

Check the incision site daily to confirm healing. Contact your vet for any signs of redness, swelling, or discharge.

Chapter 4 – Developmental Milestones and What to Expect

The puppy stage in a dog's life typically starts from birth up to 12 months of age. At this time, a series of rapid changes in growth and development occur, and for a first-time pet-owner, this can be a very overwhelming time. In order to help you cope and eventually create a lasting bond with your puppy as he grows into adulthood, you need to understand these processes.

There are five stages in the growth and development of puppies and each one comes with its own particular care requirement.

From birth to four weeks of age

When your puppy is born, he is immediately thrust into a world where only his mother and his littermates are there for him. Thus, the basic needs of the puppy need to be addressed at this time. You may see the litter constantly huddle together and this is because puppies are usually seeking warmth and protection. Pet owners usually allow the mothers to do this themselves, but if she is separated from her litter at an earlier time, you may need to step in and keep the pups fed and warm. Sensations of taste and touch are already present at birth, but it won't be until around the second or fourth week that their eyes begin to show signs of opening. As they develop their sharp sense of hearing and smell, their baby teeth also begin to break out.

From four weeks to three months old

Puppies are ready to be weaned and go home with you by around eight weeks. If he has had enough time to bond with his mother and littermates, he will have developed adequate social skills. Physical coordination may still be clumsy at times, but he is learning the ropes slowly but surely. Bite inhibition should have developed as well, especially if he used to having siblings around. Early signs of wariness to new people and strangers may show, so it is best that you reinforce positive training in order to help him cope with fear. You can also schedule your first vet visit at around this time.

From three months to six months of age

All puppies feel the need to chew, and this is a normal part of teething. By chewing, they are relieving the irritation in the gums. Puppy-proof your home during this teething stage if you don't want your stuff to get chewed up. Provide enjoyable rubber chew toys that are safe for your puppy to munch on as a non-destructive alternative.

Social standing may start to hold greater importance at this time, as social relationships become clearer. Your dog may start to become territorial and in a multi-dog household, they may learn their place in the pack.

From six months to nine months of age

Consider this time as the start of your puppy's sexual awakening. They are basically teenagers at this time, and hormones may start flying off the radar. It is at this time that you should decide whether you want to get them spayed or neutered. As they continue with their sense of self-discovery, expect them to reinforce their status in the household.

From six to 12 months

Larger breeds will continue to act like puppies until they are 18 months old, while smaller breeds should have been matured socially by 12 months old. They will sometimes push and test boundaries and will eventually settle in their own place in the pack. Cherish this time with your growing puppy by continuously engaging in play and fun activities. They will grow more in love and happiness and be the best adult dogs they can be with your guidance and training.

Chapter 5 – Socialisation for Your Puppy

Meeting other Dogs

Have your puppy and dog meet on neutral ground. Praise the adult dog when they react calmly. Keep your puppy under control and don't let him chase other pets. Make sure both dogs have separate personal items and don't ever leave them unsupervised.

Cat friends

Put the puppy in a crate and let your cat sniff him out. When both are free, keep the puppy under control and on a leash. Praise your puppy when he ignores the cat (an integral part of BAT – Behaviour Adjustment Training). If he tries to chase the cat, have him sit and distract him. Never leave the two unsupervised.

Dogs and Children

- Provide a safe retreat for your puppy that is off-limits to kids.

- Ask toddlers to practice petting a stuffed toy before introducing the puppy.

- Explain to the kids that high-pitched screaming voices can scare the puppy off.

- Challenge the kids to ignore the puppy at first. The puppy's curiosity will eventually get the better of him and he will likely approach first.

- While sitting on the floor, the child should gently toss a treat to the dog. Make sure the treat gets eaten on the floor and not on the child's hands.

- You can teach your child small duties such as refilling the water bowl, as long as he or she is supervised. The more pleasant experiences they have with the puppy, the stronger their bond becomes.

Caring for a singleton puppy

Early experiences are critical for social development, and puppies have the best chance for normal social development if they are allowed to be with their littermates at age seven to eight weeks. But in some instances, dams give birth to only one puppy.

Typical problems of singleton puppies are lack of bite inhibition, being unable to get out of trouble calmly, inability to diffuse social tension and handle frustration, the lack of social skills and impulse control, and touch sensitivity.

Work on teeth and bite inhibition as early as possible and handle a puppy with touch sensitivity often. Any regular, gentle handling is advisable. Push the puppy off the nipple once or twice a feeding to get him used to interruptions and handling the resulting frustration.

Have the puppy spend time with puppies of the same age a lot as much as possible. If possible, consider raising the puppy with another litter. Getting to spend a lot of time with another litter lets the singleton puppy have a more typical and normal experience growing up. Make sure the puppy is occupied and never bored. They should be given more opportunities to play with others.

How to Overcome Fear

Many sounds, places, and things may trigger worry and anxiety in your pet. In most cases, it is understandable as in the case of a stranger approaching; but sometimes, these fears are irrational. Your puppy may have a mild fear response such as trembling or hiding. Other times, reactions may be as severe as losing control and potentially harming others. Here are several tips to help your puppy overcome fear:

- If you see your dog in distress, the natural reaction may be to comfort him. Unfortunately, this reaction may be understood as a reward in your dog's eyes. They may feel encouraged to continue this display of fearful behaviour. Instead of comforting, try to be as calm as possible. Don't reward nor punish his behaviour and remain neutral.

- Expose your puppy to the fear in a controlled setting. If your pet is scared of a certain noise, help her overcome it by desensitising her. This involves exposing her to that noise where you are there beside her. It is also safer to work with a behaviour specialist or dog trainer for this.

- Discuss any fears or phobias your dog seems to have with a vet who knows you and your dog.

- Keep everything fun for your puppy. Puppies look to you for security and they see how you react to a situation. Keep treats handy and allow others to give these treats to your puppy.

Remember that your puppy's fear is real to him and he needs you to help him deal with it. You can help to create an environment for him that fosters self-confidence and reduce his fear, making both your lives easier and for everyone else.

Chapter 6 – Training Exercises

Good puppy manners don't come naturally. As such, you have the responsibility to teach your new pup how to behave. Use reward-based training methods, by giving them a treat when they behave well, reinforcing positive behaviour. With this, they are likely to repeat the action.

Positive Reinforcement and Reward System

One of the most effective ways to train puppies and pets, in general, is through positive reinforcement training. This is done by letting your dog know the difference between what is correct behavior from an incorrect one with the use of a reward. To ensure the training is carried out correctly, a marker is used after the correct behaviour is done. This marker can be in the form of a clicker or saying a short and simple word such as "good" or "yes." Puppies will associate with patterns very quickly and these markers help confirm which action generated the reward.

Rewards can be treats or food that the puppy loves. At other times, the reward can be anything – a toy, a praise, or a few minutes of play – as long as your puppy will be motivated enough to work for it. This type of conditioning is called positive reinforcement and is the path you want to go down in order to foster a loving relationship (as opposed to negative reinforcement which gets the same desired outcome, but through fear).

Basic Housetraining Steps

Most puppies will not be housetrained when you bring them home. Take your puppy out frequently, after every meal and nap, before bed and as soon as you get up in the morning. In the beginning, take your puppy to the same place so he can recognise his scent. Congratulate your puppy for eliminating outside. Go outside with him and give immediate praise with your voice and a pat.

If your puppy turns round and round or sniffs the floor indoors, they need to go. But don't wait for your puppy to signal to you that they want to go out. Most puppies will not learn to signal until they learn to hold it in the house first. Never punish or reprimand a puppy that has had an accident. Find ways to prevent your puppy from eliminating indoors instead. Confine the puppy to one or two rooms in the house where the family spends most time in.

If they do still keep doing their business indoors, consider investing in puppy pads. These are like nappies that soak up moisture and provide an additional scent which makes it more probable for puppies to eliminate on.

How to stop your puppy from barking

A barking puppy can disturb neighbours, especially when living in an apartment. Teach your puppy good habits from the start in order to minimise this.

Do not give your puppy attention when he barks, as even negative attention is deemed as a reward in the eyes of a dependent puppy. Some breeds are born barkers. If they persist, wait for a gap in between barking and distract the puppy with a squeaky toy, then call the dog over and train them to pick up the toy. With a toy in their mouth, they're less likely to bark. Now you can reward them for carrying the toy. Pretty soon, your puppy will learn to pick up a toy instead of barking.

Toilet and Crate Training

Potty Training

It is important that your puppy knows the right place to go to the toilet. Start by watching your puppy closely and limit their chances to pee indoors. If your puppy squats, whisk them straight outside. When you can't watch your puppy, leave them in a crate. Wait until your puppy chooses to squat on the designated toilet spot. As soon as he does this, say the cue word "toilet" and give him a treat.

Every time your puppy toilets this way, reward him. They will soon associate peeing in that spot with earning themselves a reward.

Crate Training

A crate is a safe place or den for your puppy. Choose one that will allow just enough space for your pup to lie down comfortably, without cramping his legs even when outstretched. If it is any bigger, he may decide to pee in the corner.

To facilitate comfort, provide a cloth or item that has the scent of his mother or littermates. Never force a puppy to go inside a crate. Lure him with treats instead, and if he goes inside to sniff them out, give him words of appreciation. You can also start small by allowing your puppy to eat his meal inside the crate. He will eventually feel that the crate is a safe place to be.

Eventually, your puppy will go inside the crate on his own accord. As soon as this happens, close the door. Praise the puppy again. Open the door and close back again continuously, extending the time the door remains shut. Give continuous praise.

Puppies can cry, and if he does this while being inside the crate, don't let him out immediately. This will only reinforce his behaviour. Instead, open the door of the crate once he has calmed down and reduced his crying. Do not leave your puppy inside the crate for more than 4 hours at a time. Make sure never to use the crate as punishment either or the puppy will have a negative association with it.

Teething and Bite Inhibition

How to stop your puppy from chewing your stuff

Puppies need to chew, so the trick is getting them to chew on their toys, and not on your stuff. To do this, provide an outlet for them to chew on, like giving them toys. A bored puppy can chew a lot, so entertain them with play and exercise.

Sleep Training

During the first night or two, your puppy will be feeling anxious without his mom and siblings. Puppies are usually stripped away from their mothers at only eight weeks old and deprived of the bonding they would have with them. But with a little foresight, planning, and commitment to training, you can have your puppy sleeping well throughout the night in just a few days.

Preparing for Bed

Having set routines can help prepare your puppy for sleep and give him something positive to associate with during bedtime. Exercise or play with your puppy a few hours before bedtime in order to tire him out and make him look forward to sleepy time. Your puppy will most likely sleep through the night if they have been tired out the whole day.

Due to their development, puppies are typically unable to hold their urine for more than a few hours at a time. If your puppy can do his business before bedtime, allow him to. Put away his food and water bowls at least 2 hours before bedtime. Playing classical music before and during bedtime can help soothe your puppy from whining due to the anxiety he may experience. It also helps in drowning out other sounds that are unfamiliar which may upset or arouse your puppy.

If possible, place a towel or stuffed animal in the crate that has the scent of his mom and littermates on it. A puppy explores the world with his nose first, so providing a familiar scent will help calm him down. You may also want to include a toy or cloth with the new family member's scent on to help your puppy get acquainted and comfortable with you.

Teaching Commands and Respect

You can start training with simple commands when your puppy is eight weeks old in the form of a game. At 12 weeks old, your puppy will be able to focus better.

Sit

Hold a treat above and at the front of the puppy's nose. Slowly raise your arm with the treat over the head of your puppy. The puppy will keep his eyes on the treat as it moves above him; in order to get a full view of your hand and the treats within, he will have to sit down. Once he does, mark the behavior with a clicker or the word "sit." Immediately give your puppy the treat after. Repeat this until your puppy sits on command.

Stay

Command your dog to sit. Wait for a few seconds before giving your puppy the treat. After this pause, mark the behavior with a clicker or a cue word, "stay." Allow him to sit still, and then take one step away. Go back to his side again. Repeat this, gradually adding the distance between the both of you.

Come

Start by staying away from your puppy. They will naturally feel the need to get close to you and follow where you are. When he begins to advance towards you, say, "Come," in a high-pitched and excited voice. Once he arrives next to you, give him a treat.

Walking with a leash

Do not allow your puppy to lead. Instead, walk forward while guiding him beside you. If he starts to run ahead, stop and call his attention. If he starts to change the direction, don't let him. Move him in the opposite direction so that he will know you are solely in charge.

Conclusion

Having a canine companion to call your own can give immeasurable happiness, no doubt. But with it comes the challenges of rearing and raising a puppy to adulthood. And just as it takes a whole village to raise a child, it also takes commitment, effort, and time to raise a puppy.

As a first-timer, this can be daunting and overwhelming, but the reward of seeing your puppy grow into a lovable and loyal companion is definitely worth it. So, hang in there, and know that you got this!

Dear Reader,

Thanks for exploring this book with me. Now that you know how to raise the perfect puppy…

…could you kindly leave a review on the link below?

Thanks,

Max

P.S. Reviews are like giving a warm hug to your favorite author.

We love hugs.

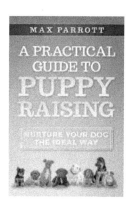

https://www.amazon.com/dp/B07GCXY67H

Also, if you would like a list of free audiobooks, please be sure to Like our Facebook Page and send a message to claim them:

https://www.facebook.com/RylstonePublishing/

Check Out Other Books

https://www.amazon.com/dp/B081TW5J5B

ation can be obtained
ing.com
iA
420
B/1222